CATE MORRIS

BEYOND THE SIEGE

WALKING AWAY FROM THE ENEMY

CATE MORRIS

BEYOND THE SIEGE

WALKING AWAY FROM THE ENEMY

IGLOO TUNES
Publishing

BEYOND THE SIEGE: *Walking Away from the Enemy*

FIRST EDITION
Igloo Tunes Publishing

ISBN-10:978-0-578-74700-2
ISBN-13:978-0-578-74700-2

Scripture quotations marked "NIV" are taken from The
Holy Bible, New International Version® NIV® Copyright
© 1973, 1978, 1984 by International Bible Society® Used
by permission.

Author website: www.catemorris.com

Photography: Laural Sabin at
www.lauralsabinphotography.com

Editing: Amy Jo Barton at www.ajbwriting.com

Cover Design: David Stoddard, Media Revelation, at
www.mediarevelation.com

Publishing: Marie Fowler, Maon Media at
www.allgloriouswithincom.wordpress.com

DEDICATION

I would like to dedicate this book to my mom; my brother, Stan; and my sister, Promise. We all lived through a siege, and we continue to walk toward hope and healing. May this book be another reminder that our story is still being written in love, grace, healing, hope, and redemption.

And to my children, may you always remember that you + God = an army.

SIEGE:

1. A military blockade of a city or fortified place to compel it to surrender.
2. A persistent or serious attack (Merriam-Webster).

TABLE OF CONTENTS

ENDORSEMENTS

"A timely book for our day and age as we are besieged with negative thoughts and destructive messages. Cate does a beautiful job of sharing how she became an overcomer using godly principles and shares that wisdom with us."
                              - Pastor Rick Bonnette

"The message in this book, when taken to heart and applied, has the capability to be transformative! Are you tired of feeling alone and desperate for connection? Take the step of faith and choose to believe what God says is true. Align yourself with what he says, and just wait, because your miracle of hope and freedom is coming!"
                              -Dori Hagen, MA, LPC

"Cate's vulnerability in sharing life experiences intersects with biblical truth in a way that is uplifting and encouraging. She challenges us to analyze our thought patterns and weigh them against Scripture, allowing God's word to change our paradigm."
                              -Sarah Coke

"Cate's message of hope is especially timely. The honesty and wisdom with which she writes is sure to inspire faith and life in those who take it to heart."
    –Eric Rozeboom, President, Alaska Bible Institute

"Cate's writing is vulnerable, authentic, and encouraging. Nearly every page is full of practical wisdom and revelation into our unhealthy thoughts, temptations, and struggles. She brings hope, clarity, and inspiration into subjects that can seem discouraging, confusing, or overwhelming. This is a must-read for those who find themselves filled with thoughts of shame or disappointment. The Holy Spirit will breathe life and expectation into your mind as you read."
    - Nathan Steel, Director of Cultivate

ACKNOWLEDGEMENTS

With sincere gratitude and appreciation, I want to thank . . .

Jesus, who loved me as he found me. I first met him as a five year old in need of a Savior, and he continues to write my story with his redemption.

My mom, Cecelia Schwartz, who was the anchor through my difficult years and still champions my faith and walk to freedom.

My husband, Jamin, for being one of my biggest defenders and my compassionate partner in life; and my children—Bethany, Jaron, Chad, and Melanie, who have believed in me and cheered me on through many projects.

My dear friends who encouraged me to write because they believed I had something to say that needed to be said--Manuel Luz, Laural Sabin, Theresa Engebretsen, and Nan Porter. Thank you for contributing and cheering me on through the writing process; Amy Barton, my childhood friend and book editor, for helping my words and thoughts say what needed to be said in concise and grammatically correct ways.

Darren Lindley, whose message on the "Four Lepers" became the catalyst to my freedom and the inspiration of this book.

Marie Fowler, who put my thoughts to print and partnered in prayer with me for this project; David Stoddard, who designed my cover and listened closely to my vision; and Rick Bonnette, for contributing his lessons learned to my life and to this book.

INTRODUCTION

THE SIEGE OF MY MIND

I lay there, curled up in a ball on the floor of our bedroom closet—shoes beneath me, clothes dangling above—completely unaware of the physical discomfort. Despair entrenched me. I cried in agony; my whole body ached, and my imagination took center stage. Thoughts and images flashed through my mind in a continuous loop. *Here are ways you can kill yourself,* they whispered. The feelings of hopelessness felt familiar, like a heavy weight on my mind, and an urgency to end it all began to torment me.

Months of loss culminated in that one day: A friend I thought I had connected with in meaningful ways called to let me know she was dropping me from her life. My marriage continued to struggle from years of financial strain and associated stress. Our family moved, once again, from one city to another for work. I could not seem to propel myself forward with the pain I felt.

There seemed to be no end in sight.

Looking back, I don't recall what happened that particular day to trigger suicidal thoughts. I only know the cumulative incidents of untended pain came crashing down on me, and I felt myself being pulled under by a despair that threatened no escape.

It began in childhood. An abusive father and the painful family dynamic he created fostered a sense of hopelessness. Despite temporary reprieves, I saw hope as futile. I couldn't escape—ultimate help was out of reach. Just like that, the enemy began his siege of my mind. Seeds planted in those childhood beliefs grew into choking weeds in my adult years. I learned to survive the wars of my adolescent years, yet I never grew dull to the enemy's voices and threats. They became a part of me in ways I didn't understand.

There I was, a mother of four, with more blessings than I could count, allowing misery and suicide to cloud my view of the present and the future. I desperately needed to escape their grip on my mind.

> "Stop, Cate. Reflect for a minute. Don't go down this path."

Then it happened. A flash of memory: I sat in a church sanctuary, listening to Daren Lindley preach on the siege of Samaria from 2 Kings; as he spoke, the Holy Spirit's voice took over, calling out my suicidal battles and the thoughts that led me into them.

That memory jolted me and gave me the strength needed to change my direction. The journey that followed is what this book is about. It's a story of rising and falling, of letting go of lies and clinging tenaciously to hope. It's how I learned to question my thoughts before they become actions—because actions cannot be reversed, and the consequences of those actions fall on others as well.

It's the story of how I learned that even when I feel hopeless, I have decisions to make, and those decisions will either lead me to mercy or to death. It's how I learned that when I am most tempted to throw precious things away, I need a bold courage to change my course of action. And it's how these lessons became the catalyst for developing a team I can call on when afraid—a team who will pray for me and encourage my steps toward help.

While I've learned a lot along the way regarding how to cope with life's disappointments, my story continues to unfold. I hope to take you with me on this journey.

As I write, I picture you: Maybe you're battling hopelessness and despair or know someone who is. Maybe you don't know what to do and are being tempted with a quick fix that will ultimately destroy you or something precious to you.

In the pages of this book, I want you to see the direction despair will take you. I want you to hear your enemy's voice and begin to distinguish it from your own.

More than that, I want you to hear your maker, your father God who speaks hope, healing, deliverance, and restoration. His voice is calling you out of your depression and despair and beckoning you his direction. I want you to look confidently into the eyes of the one who knows what to do and knows how to deliver you. Repentance is a turning—turning away from the voice of the enemy, turning to the voice of God, to hear it clearer and believe what he says.

I pray the Holy Spirit might use 2 Kings 6 and 7 as a catalyst for your healing, as well—that you might believe in a life worth living, one that goes beyond our current battles and outlives our adversary.

1

THE SIEGE BEGINS

s a child, I was my father's favorite—the baby girl. With one older brother almost three years my senior and another in heaven, I was the grand finale (or so my parents thought; my little sister arrived thirteen years later).

It didn't take long to notice how my dad treated my mother. If he wasn't overpowering her physically, he was using his words to make her feel unlovely, rejected, small, and insignificant. He would take her car keys, block exits, or lock her in the house, forbidding her to leave and threatening her if she did.

He lived in constant fear of losing power.

No doubt that's why my older brother became his next target. After all, boys grow up to be men, and men overpower other men. So, my dad devised a plan to ensure his son would never succeed at manhood by using the same methods used on my mother: he belittled him, gave him chore after chore, bullied him, held back his approval, and rarely showed him affection. He was determined to remain dominant and keep my brother subordinate.

To give you an idea, my dad liked to hug me in front of the rest of the family. While he held me, he barked orders to my brother; while he "loved" me, he belittled my brother and called him a failure. This scenario played out time and time again before I could take it no longer. Being dad's favorite meant praise for me but pain and hardship for my brother and my mom.

So, I formulated a plan to ensure the tide would turn.

I would stop hugging my dad. If he didn't get hugs from me, he would reach out to my brother and be kinder to my mom; he would notice the deficit of love and realize he needed to do something about it. Once he noticed the loss, I mused, he would begin hugging my brother and loving my mother—then everything would be even, and I could begin hugging him again. It was a perfect plan.

Of course, I soon discovered you can't force love. You can't manipulate kindness out of someone who doesn't want to give it. You can only strengthen the fear of losing power by changing your role.

That's when the tables began to turn.

My dad saw my lack of affection as rejection of him, which began to complicate and compound his insecurities. He tried to get back what I withheld. I wouldn't budge. He became angry. I received his wrath. And although I hated how he treated me, a certain satisfaction arose from knowing my mother and brother were no longer alone. Now we were all on the same playing field.

But in the sixth grade I first uttered the words, "I think I am depressed."

My parents were separating because of my father's angry, abusive behavior. While necessary, as a child I wanted their restoration more. My heart was battered and broken from the despair in which we lived—the abuse and the separation seemed to say things would not get better. The prospect of a good life began to falter. Depression filled me with hopelessness and the siege began. The enemy who comes only to kill, steal, and destroy worked feverishly to demolish my hope.

A few months later, my parents got back together, hoping to work things out. Unfortunately, my father's cycle of verbal, physical, and emotional abuse began again. The anger and pain ate away at my desire to live. As a child, I had no power over the situation. There didn't seem to be any physical escape. I feared losing those closest to me; and ironically, I feared losing my own life even more, knowing the pain it would inflict on others. Yet suicide's seductive voice swept into our family and began tempting us all.

For reasons only God could orchestrate, none of us could bring ourselves to go through with it. Instead, I entertained thoughts of dying over and over. For hours I meditated on the most effective ways to end my life. My thoughts became so entrenched in death, sometimes I longed to be murdered so my death would not have to come by my own hands. I envisioned myself a victim of horrendous crimes, where relief would come once my life was extinguished.

This perverted way of thinking somehow comforted me in the midst of pain. At the same time, I felt so ashamed because I knew my thoughts weren't healthy; but in my despair, peace was a state of mind I thought I had to manufacture. Shame quickly hijacked my identity.

"Your existence causes problems and pain for others."

Like a broken record, this message looped in my head all my life. Somehow, with each statement, my mind produced photos and memories of instances in my life that seemed to validate those words and solidify my belief in their truth.

I reasoned that if my existence creates pain, then my non-existence should remove that pain. My siege was in full force. For the next thirty years, I felt trapped in hopelessness whenever the stresses of life climbed higher. Like a city surrounded by an enemy, I became a victim to the lies that kept me locked in despair.

I didn't see it coming; I had no idea what the enemy was building in my life all those years. It seemed logical to believe it was just a tough life that wasn't working out for me. The famine of hope had set in before I realized it was dwindling. And that's just how the enemy had planned it. Gradual, calculated, determined, and strategic, he slowly built his armament against me and led me to believe I was trapped. If I continued cooperating with his plan, I would surely self-destruct.

To be truly set free, I needed to look hopelessness in the eyes and see my own reflection. If I was really going to fight, I needed to fight with my eyes wide open. My operating assumptions needed to be exposed; my imagination needed a flush.

And I found a catalyst in 2 Kings.

In that particular setting, two women and four lepers stand in the spotlight. Prolonged threats from outside the city gates, combined with the famine within, created hopelessness, propelling them to make choices.

You see, the Arameans, an ancient enemy kingdom to Israel, knew how a siege worked best. They wouldn't have to break down the walls of a fortified city if they could succeed in breaking down the wills of those inside.

The choices made by those women and men made history. I have come to learn that our choices make history too.

2

FAMINE IN THE LAND

J oram, the son of Ahab and Jezebel, had a very frustrating reign as king over the Northern Kingdom of Israel in Samaria. Like his parents before him, Joram wanted to be the supreme ruler over Israel without a relationship with the God who formed, rescued, and preserved that nation. He even resented that God gave wisdom to the prophet Elisha, because it forced him to listen to a man of God for insight.

Maybe he mirrored what his parents modeled, maybe he decided for himself; whatever the story, King Joram lived with a chip on his shoulder regarding God and his prophets. It was convenient to blame them for any negative consequences that resulted from his own poor decisions.

For at least seven years, a famine assailed the land of Israel and Samaria. Attempting to use the famine to their advantage, enemy armies of the nation of Aram planned several attacks on Israel. Miraculously, many of their raids were foiled because God revealed their strategies to the prophet Elisha, who in turn alerted King Joram.

But when God warned King Joram and he refused to listen, God did not intervene. King Ben-Hadad, the king of Aram, mobilized his entire army to lay siege on Samaria—and this time he succeeded.[1]

Ben-Hadad's army used intimidation to help execute their siege: they paraded their military strength; they shouted threats. Then they backed up their threats with actions. They succeeded at cutting off the flow of goods and services coming into and going out of Samaria, a strategy that exacerbated the conditions of the famine within Samaria's walls and left Israel in dire circumstances with rapidly dwindling resources.

The army of Aram's goal was to let starvation begin to force Israel's hand in surrender, and the strategy was working. Food became so scarce within the city walls, people ate the dung of doves and butchered their service animals, eating every edible part. Any kind of sustenance sold for an exorbitant price, leaving the inhabitants without the ability to buy anything to eat. We are told "the siege lasted so long that a donkey's head sold for eighty shekels[2] of silver, and a quarter of a cab[3] of seed pods[4] for five shekels.[5]

Aram's military threat was real. It was not a figment of Israel's imagination; however, the effects of this siege began to work their way into the minds of the victims in ways even Ben-Hadad couldn't have predicted.

---

[1] 2 Kings 6:24 NIV

[2] About 1 kilogram
[3] About 0.3 liter
[4] From doves' dung

[5] 2 Kings 6:25

As hopelessness and despair dug in its talons, the imaginations of men and women twisted and succumbed to its devastation. The consequences of this siege on Samaria became incalculable and unconscionable as the hope of those living within the walls of the city dissipated.

It's not as if they hadn't been warned. Generations before, Moses forewarned the Israelites of what would happen if they decided to shift their trust from God to idols:

> *The Lord will bring a nation against you from far away, from the ends of the earth, like an eagle swooping down, a nation whose language you will not understand, a fierce-looking nation without respect for the old or pity for the young. They will devour the young of your livestock and the crops of your land until you are destroyed. They will leave you no grain, new wine or olive oil, nor any calves of your herds or lambs of your flocks until you are ruined. They will lay siege to all the cities throughout your land until the high fortified walls in which you trust fall down. They will besiege all the cities throughout the land the Lord your God is giving you. Because of the suffering your enemy will inflict on you during the siege, you will eat the fruit of the womb, the flesh of the sons and daughters the Lord your God has given you. Even the most gentle and sensitive man among you will have no compassion on his own brother or the wife he loves or his surviving children, and he will not give to one of them any of the flesh of his children that he is eating.*

It will be all he has left because of the
suffering your enemy will inflict on you
during the siege of all your cities. The most
gentle and sensitive woman among you—so
sensitive and gentle that she would not
venture to touch the ground with the sole of
her foot—will begrudge the husband she
loves and her own son or daughter the after
birth from her womb and the children she
bears. For in her dire need she intends to eat
them secretly because of the suffering your
enemy will inflict on you during the siege of
your cities.[7]

Just as Moses warned, two women with sons in the city of
Samaria made a last-ditch effort for survival; they struck a
deal with each other that would reveal how hopelessness,
once internalized, destroys. We learn of this gruesome story
and how it played out when one pleads with King Joram for
justice:

As the king of Israel was passing by on the
wall, a woman cried to him, "Help me, my
lord the king!" The king replied, "If the
Lord does not help you, where can I get help
for you? From the threshing floor? From the
winepress?" Then he asked her, "What's the
matter?" She answered, *"This woman said*
to me, 'Give up your son so we may eat him
today, and tomorrow we'll eat my son.' So,
we cooked my son and ate him. The next
day I said to her, 'Give up your son so we
may eat him,' but she had hidden him."

[7] Deut. 28:49–53

*When the king heard the woman's words, he
tore his robes. As he went along the wall,
the people looked, and they saw that, under
his robes, he had sackcloth on his body.*[8]

Until you experience hopelessness, you really cannot
imagine the options for escape the enemy will parade in
front of you. So many ideas can boast of relieving your
pain but ultimately end in addiction, isolation, and death. In
a famine, feces become a feast and anything you value
quickly becomes a bartering chip for a fix.

Desperation has a way of blurring the lines of the
precious and the temporary fix like nothing else can. As
this story illustrates so well, values can quickly become
subjective and the profane can be served up as a banquet.
The women struck a deal that left one child dead, two
stomachs churning, and a crisis of justice that could not be
resolved this side of heaven. Our enemy never offers real
hope. He can't. There's no hope in him.

The siege not only happened on the outside walls of the
city of Samaria, it infiltrated the minds of its inhabitants—
even the king. King Joram became over-wrought with the
news the woman brought him. Things had been bad in his
city, but this—this reeked of despair that rots the soul. He
had no answers. He tore his clothes in anguish.

How could a mother agree to give up her own son to
cannibalism? Did it seem more merciful to kill her child
swiftly rather than watch him languish in starvation and die
as many around them had already done? Did she reason he
was near dead anyway and his body could save the lives of
others? Did she attempt to back out or otherwise question
her decision?

[8] 2 Kings 6:26–30

We do not know the thoughts that went through her head; we cannot answer for her choices. We can, however, answer for our own. The Holy Spirit can help us turn those questions inward to investigate our own hopeless thoughts.

ENCIRCLED

Growing up in a home with physical, verbal, and emotional abuse, there are things I heard and experienced repetitively. The combination of threats and painful actions, compounded over sixteen years, formed a framework of fear in which I lived.

The enemy always seemed near—and powerful. He convinced me I was always a victim. Anything that triggered my fear left me feeling trapped, even when I had options for help. Once I believed there was no hope, it made it easier for Satan to convince me I needed to stop the merry-go-round of my life by ending it. Satan was the one marching in circles around my mind, but he convinced me I too was stuck in those circles.

Perhaps you can relate. Perhaps you too know what it's like for thoughts to run endless circles, to believe you can't break free. Your mind is stuck on "repeat." Your thoughts are hopeless, and your emotions join the dirge. No matter how much you want to think about something else, your thoughts travel the well-worn path of fear, stress, anxiety, discouragement, doubt, anger, and bitterness.

You may describe it as a spinning vortex of despair or liken it to an endless broken record. I call it a siege. Like the warriors of the armies of Aram circling the city of Samaria, the enemy marches his lies in a circle around our thoughts until he's captured our imaginations.

When we begin to feel hopeless and caught in something inescapable, that's when we're prone to believe his lies, because they're on a constant broadcast. And it's in our weakest moments the enemy attempts to strike the most damaging of deals.

DESPERATION

When our thoughts are discouraging, when the music we listen to, the conversations we have, and the news we let into our hearts only speak of pain and hardship, we begin to despair. Despair is an utter loss of hope.[9] A loss of all hope becomes a famine of the soul that depletes our energy. We lose the will to fight, to create solutions, or to alter our course. This in turn can create feelings of panic that compel us to make quick decisions that look good in the short-term but aren't always good for the long-term.

Always looking for an opportune time, Satan often introduces his destructive thoughts at the stage of our siege when we feel like we are out of solutions. He does this in hopes that we will think his thoughts are our own ideas and will act on them. Once we entertain and internalize his thoughts, the actions that flow from them become our responsibility.

The thing is, desperation settles in through many avenues. Some of our most painful experiences are not great, repetitive events; they're seemingly small, isolated moments that take on fearful lives of their own . . .

"No one will ever want you."

---

[9] *Merriam-Webster.com Dictionary*, s.v. "despair," accessed March 5, 2020, https://www.merriam-webster.com/dictionary/despair.

That was said to me only once, but it took root in my adolescent soul and became an imaginary army that marched around my identity for years. I believed it. The enemy planted that lie and walked away. My imagination took it from there.

That's the enemy's strategy. He starts a campaign of fear, through lies, that continues to encircle our minds. Once we internalize the fear, he can walk away for hours, days, even years, certain we'll be too afraid to "leave the city." It's a brilliant form of warfare that can take decades to recognize.

If successful, the enemy's lies sound like our own thoughts. He'll tell half-truths, threaten with retaliation, and even flat-out lie to control our identities and decisions. When our own self-talk sounds like self-cursing, it's an indicator that we have adopted lies and made them our own thoughts.

Sadly, in a siege, we tend to want to fight against hope, resist help, and cower from our strengths; we lean into our weaknesses and give up. If we don't have truth speaking into our pain, we'll live in a famine that eats away at our resolve and ultimately our humanity. Truth may be all around us, but the siege keeps it from fully reaching our hearts.

"If we don't have truth speaking into our pain, we'll live in a famine that eats away at our resolve and ultimately our humanity. "

The two women from 2 Kings 6 allowed despair and hopelessness to cloud their vision and muddle their thinking. Desperation tempted them with a damaging escape and a deconstructed hope. We are horrified by their decisions. At times, we should be horrified by our own.

3

AWOL

I n order to recognize where the enemy has captured our imaginations, we must understand our purpose and why we were created. For example, I can use a smartphone as a spade in my garden with a certain amount of effectiveness. But my violation of the phone's purpose causes me and the phone to fall short of the "glory" for which it was designed. Unless I know the objective of the smartphone, I cannot know the joys of utilizing its many functions.

Similarly, unless we understand the purposes for which we have been made, we will not experience the joys intended for us, nor will we comprehend the consequences of our violations against God and one another. We must know how God sees us and what he desires for us, then join our hearts and thoughts with his.

Thankfully, we can trace our purpose back to the very beginning where God set his intentions. The Bible tells us God created humanity in his image—his very breath made us alive.[1] Fashioned by God out of his heart of love, we were designed to be the praise and glory of our creator.

[1] Gen. 1:27 and 2:7

Scripture tells us that the first man and woman, Adam and Eve, shared a daily fellowship with God. He walked with them, talked with them, and from his wisdom, he instructed them in all areas of life. From the garden where they lived, they were to be fruitful, multiply, and fill the whole earth.[2] This was to be our heritage too. A life lived in the presence of God—enjoying the fullness of all he created for us.

But Satan had other ideas.

Lucifer, a beautiful, magnificent angel whose pride and desire for worship turned him against God, was kicked out of heaven along with those who sided with him.[3] Trading his heavenly glory for pride, Lucifer, whose name meant "son of the morning,"[4] became known as Satan, "adversary."[5] Maybe for revenge, maybe to gain more authority against God, Satan decided to make mankind the target for destruction.

> In the words of Jesus,
> *"He was a murderer from the beginning, not holding to the truth, for there is no truth in him. When he lies, he speaks his native language, for he is a liar and the father of lies."*[6]

---

[2] Gen. 1:28

[3] It's generally believed that one third of heaven's angels fell, based on Revelation 12:4: "And his tail swept away a third of the stars of heaven, and threw them to the earth. And the dragon stood before the woman who was about to give birth, so that when she gave birth, he might devour her child."

[4] Roswell D. Hitchcock, "Lucifer" in An Interpreting Dictionary of Scripture Proper Names (New York, 1869).

[5] Walter A. Elwell, "Satan" in Evangelical Dictionary of Theology, Grand Rapids, Michigan Baker Book House Company, ,1997.

[6] John 8:44b

What could be more painful than destroying the people God created and loves? To accomplish his plan, Satan's chief aim is to separate us from truth so we might be candidates for destruction.

You see, there's nothing in Scripture that suggests an omnipresent or omniscient enemy. Satan's power in and over us must be granted to him. Therefore, it should come as no surprise that one of the most powerful weapons he uses against us is a lie. It only takes one to separate us from God. But Satan doesn't take chances.

Over the course of a lifetime, he'll plant lie after lie, like landmines. Satan will utilize any avenue available to plant his thoughts: family, friends, enemies, media, false religions, world events, life circumstances. His suggestions and impressions in themselves have no real power. They are lies, after all. But when we begin believing those lies, Satan gains authority. Sadly, most of us are guilty of handing over our authority at one point or another.

GENERATIONAL CONSEQUENCES

Wes Stafford recalls the story of an old man he encountered in poverty-stricken Haiti. The man was chopping down a mango tree so he could turn it into charcoal, all to make seventy-five dollars for his family. Stafford tried to reason with him: killing the tree would be a bad idea because it was the only living thing for miles; it was still producing a crop of mangos that could be sold twice a year for seventy-five dollars each. The man dismissed the idea and continued chopping. Feeling frantic to argue his point, Stafford grabbed the old man's machete wielding hand and implored him:

"Don't you see? If you kill it now . . .

'No, don't you see?!' he suddenly shouted at me, his eyes brimming with tears, 'I don't know that my children or I will even be alive five months from now! All we have is today. I barely have that!'

I stood and watched his rhythmic chopping for a while longer. Behind his hand was the hand of an enemy at work. Satan's fingerprints were all over the tragedy I was witnessing."[7]

When we're in the grip of a siege, hope seems out of reach. In those frantic moments, when we feel desperate to escape our fear or pain, bad decisions will masquerade as viable solutions. What we do with those thoughts can impact our hope and our lives. It can impact generations to come.

Ravi Zacharias often defined sin as "violating purpose."[8] You and I are created in the image of God. We are inherently gifted with value, meaning, and purpose. Our purpose is founded in and bounded by the holiness and unfailing goodness of God, who designed us according to his good pleasure.[9]

Being created by love, for love, in order to love, our lives are intended to be a continuous expression of the character of God. Anything short of God's character—lies, murder, hate, covetousness, pride, greed, unbridled anger, lust, and selfishness—violates our purpose. God calls it sin. It separates us from God and from one another.

---

[7] Wes Stafford, *Too Small to Ignore*, (Colorado, Waterbrook Press, 2005), 186–187.

[8] Ravi Zacharias, Twitter post, June 2014, 9:18 a.m., twitter.com/Ravi Zacharias/status/480731662834475008?lang=en

[9] Eph. 2:10

And the Bible tells us, "all have sinned and
fall short of the glory of God."[10]

Most wars, feuds, racism, prejudice, unforgiveness, and
bitterness of our world trace their beginnings back
generations. They may even have roots that extend all the
way back to the first man and woman.

Picture Adam and Eve in the Garden of Eden.[11] The
temptation to sin is before them; perhaps the thought
floated through their minds,

"What does it matter what we do? We're the only ones
here. It's not like we're going to hurt anyone."

If anyone had the "right" to exercise such reasoning, Adam
and Eve would be candidates. The problem, as we discover,
is that sin doesn't just hurt the sinner. It affects generations.

"We make no decision in a vacuum, free from consequences
falling on anyone else, even when we think we're all alone."

In Adam and Eve's case, the decision to believe a lie about
God's words and his nature crippled all of humanity, in
every culture and nation.

[10] Rom. 3:23 KJV
[11] Gen. 3

We make no decision in a vacuum, free from consequences falling on anyone else, even when we think we're all alone. Unfortunately, our sins against God and one another always carry forward. In the story of 2 Kings, the women ate one of their sons. An heir was killed and a lineage cut off forever. The quick decision for a meal became incalculable in its generational devastation. While the decisions we make today may not have quite this dire consequence, they'll still have consequences—they'll still impact future generations in one way or another.

"For the wages of sin is death . . ."[12]

If we don't cling to our convictions in the battle against despair, we're sure to give up something precious in trade for a "fix." Decisions made in haste, to satisfy a perceived need, result in generational consequences. When the enemy strikes a deal with us, it always causes us to lose big (like Esau, who traded his firstborn birthright to his brother in exchange for a bowl of soup.)[13] In one moment of weakness, we can be coerced into giving up that and so much more.

We must take every thought captive to the obedience of Christ.[14] It is only when we fully examine our thoughts that we are able to discern their source. It may seem like a daunting task, but with some practice we will begin to recognize our enemy.

---

[12] Rom. 6:23a KJV
[13] Gen. 25:29–34
[14] 2 Cor. 10:5 KJV

4

RECOGNIZING THE ENEMY

P aul tells us, "our struggle is not against flesh and blood, but against the rulers, against the authorities, against the powers of this dark world and against the spiritual forces of evil in the heavenly realms."[1]

As we saw in the last chapter, it's easy to be blinded to our siege. We blame our circumstances or people who have wounded us. We may even assume this is "as good as it gets" in life. By the time we realize we're surrounded by our enemy, our defenses are down, desperation has set in, and we believe all our thoughts to be our own. How can we escape ourselves? Thankfully, we don't need to; we need to escape the enemy. But first we need to recognize him.

[1] Eph. 6:12

34

OUR LITMUS TEST

To start, let's go back to the first sin, when Adam and Eve believed the doubts and lies of Satan. Satan convinced them God wasn't that good. He took a partial truth (that God warned them against eating the tree of the knowledge of good and evil) and twisted it; he told them God was holding out on them by forbidding knowledge that would make them equal to God.

Suddenly the fruit God said not to eat seemed appetizing and Adam and Eve decided to eat it. Immediately they became ashamed and afraid. They sewed fig leaves together to cover their nakedness, and then they hid.

Isn't it amazing? When Adam and Eve ate from the tree of the knowledge of good and evil, they immediately felt the consequences of sin. Their ability to recognize evil made them self-conscious and sent them scrambling for cover. Their relationship with God changed dramatically that day.

When God came to the garden in the cool of the evening, as he always did, he came with questions.[2] The two questions God asks Adam and Eve (one implied) serve as our litmus test for recognizing the enemy . . .

[2] Gen. 3

WHERE ARE YOU?

"Where are you?" God asks.

When we're feeling alone, vulnerable, scared, or guilty, we begin to hide. We may not always lock ourselves in a bedroom closet, but we no longer show up in places we used to enjoy. We may lose interest in friendships; we may be less conversational; we may find mustering the energy to get out of bed too difficult.

If you find yourself sneaking around or entertaining secret habits—when addictions suddenly sound like solutions or escapes, you know you're hiding.

So many of the "escapes" our enemy offers us become bondages to our families and to us. As Daniel Kolenda once said,

> "If you need to be delivered from an
> 'escape,' it is not an escape at all. It is a
> prison; it is a living tomb."[3]

For Adam and Eve, and for each of us, hiding and hedging becomes a prison of shame. Addictions meant to numb us become prisons. We need a Savior.

Lies will always give us a sense of guilt or shame, because the only power sin has is its secrecy. Bringing our thoughts and our whole selves out into the light of God's truth is the only path to escaping the power of sin.

---

[3] Contend Global, "Daniel Kolenda: Be Saved from this Perverse Generation," May 24, 2016, YouTube video Azusa Now Livestream- Last 4 Hours English , 2:48, www.youtube.com/watch?v=5L7q8fYuQao.

When God asked, "Where are you?" it wasn't because he lost Adam and Eve. He knew exactly where they were. He wanted them to come out from hiding. He wanted them to acknowledge the drastic change in relationship that just happened. He wants the same of us—because we must recognize our need before we are willing to reach for help.

WHO TOLD YOU?

Then God asks, "Who told you that you were naked?"

When God created Adam and Eve, it was with complete innocence and purity. They didn't know shame; they had no reason to question each other's motives, let alone the motives of their creator. So why were they ashamed and mistrusting; who taught them to be ashamed?

Who taught us to hedge, lie, avoid, and hide?

The voices or thoughts in our heads span a lifetime of input and come from a variety of sources: It may be something said by a family member or friend. It may be something you read in a magazine, viewed on the internet, saw in a movie, or heard in a song lyric.

Not everything we come to believe in our lives is supposed to be part of our identities; neither does every thought in our minds originate in us. God's voice is supposed to be our input and compass. But too often we replace many of his words with the voices of others.

When you find yourself hiding, that's when you need to take a closer look at what you're believing in that moment. Then you need to interrogate the voice that's saying it. Where did it come from and why? You may even need to grab a pen and paper to trace its origin.

Adam blamed Eve. Eve blamed the serpent. But neither could say it was God who told them they were naked. There was another voice influencing their decisions.

IS THAT SOMETHING
I WOULD SAY?

If God were to ask a follow-up question to Adam and Eve, it might be, "Were the words you listened to something I would actually say?"

God always speaks hope. When God speaks, your heart hears anticipation, faith, victory, help, and healing. When the enemy speaks, you hear fear, mistrust, defeat, alienation, and condemnation.

For example, when the enemy says,

> "You will always be this way. Things will
> never change. There is no hope."

God says, "I know about your sin, but I will redeem you. I will transform you. I will change and heal you." God's words correct without diminishing our value; he offers supernatural help to change our circumstances.

Those of us who've been Christians for any length of time know this in our heart of hearts. We've seen his power at work; we've experienced his goodness. So, Satan continues with the same tactic he's used for generations: he takes partial truths and asks, "Did God really say . . .?"

Satan desires us to doubt God's intentions, our testimonies of the goodness of God, our own abilities to hear God clearly, and even God's ability to communicate with us. In those moments of doubt, Satan throws us another script,

"Maybe reality actually looks like this . . ."

How could we come to such conclusions? How could we believe he isn't good? Why would we be so distrusting? Why on earth would we hide? Adam and Eve had to answer. You and I need to answer too.

5

DECIPHERING THE TRUTH

Recognizing our enemy often requires that we evaluate and change some systems that our minds and hearts use to interact with the world around us. Because of our imaginations, some things that appear true are powerless ideas masquerading as concrete realities. They are voices that speak to us with authority; in reality, they are subject to our approval.

Regret, shame, comparison, self-doubt, discouragement, an orphaned spirit, blame, and others all fight for prominence in our thinking. It takes some practice to recognize them, but once you do, you can call them out for what they really are.

IMAGINATION

Imagination is a powerful thing. Being made in the image of a creative God, we are endowed with creativity and purpose built into our framework. Our imaginations are capable of great inventions, brilliant discoveries, beautiful art, and purpose. Satan knows this and wants full access. If he can convince us to read his scripts, we are capable of deconstructions, perversions, and self-mutilations.

Merriam Webster defines *imagination* as: 1. The act or power of forming a mental image of something not present to the senses or never wholly perceived in reality; 2. Creative ability; 3. A creation of the mind; a fanciful or empty assumption.[1]

Imagination is more than dreaming up sci-fi stories of interstellar empires or fantastical characters the likes of unicorns or mermaids. It's also an act of the will—and it can only be played out on the stage of our minds.

Think of the mind as a theatre. The backdrop is made up of real-life situations: love, fear, or loss. Our imaginations put the characters on the stage, and we play the scenes over and over, fretting and worrying. We're just as skilled at making up scenarios we think "could" happen in our lives. Playing proposed storylines over and over, we decide what voice gets to speak the most lines (or speak loudest). We choose the villain or the hero, the winner or the loser. The drama unfolds as our imaginations create, until our minds are consumed.

In other words, you don't have to be dancing with Pegasus or talking to leprechauns to be an imaginative person. If you face your mornings with dread or stay awake at night ruminating on hypothetical drama until it unfolds into physical stress in your body, you're using your imagination. If you picture a tomorrow even darker than today, you're using your imagination.

No one has seen your tomorrow except God himself; that's why Jesus says:

> *Therefore, I tell you, do not worry about*
> *your life, what you will eat or drink; or*

---

[1] Merriam-Webster.com Dictionary, s.v. "imagination," accessed March 5, 2020, https://www.merriam-webster.com/dictionary/imagination.

*about your body, what you will wear. Is not
life more than food, and the body more than
clothes? Look at the birds of the air; they do
not sow or reap or store away in barns, and
yet your heavenly Father feeds them. Are
you not much more valuable than they?
Can any one of you by worrying add a
single hour to your life? And why do you
worry about clothes? See how the flowers of
the field grow. They do not labor or spin.
Yet I tell you that not even Solomon in all
his splendor was dressed like one of these.
If that is how God clothes the grass of the
field, which is here today and tomorrow is
thrown into the fire, will he not much more
clothe you—you of little faith? So do not
worry, saying, "What shall we eat?" or
"What shall we drink?" or "What shall we
wear?" For the pagans run after all these
things, and your heavenly Father knows that
you need them. But seek first his kingdom
and his righteousness, and all these things
will be given to you as well. Therefore, do
not worry about tomorrow, for tomorrow
will worry about itself. Each day has enough
trouble of its own.[2]*

Imagination has the power to write the scripts of our lives,
and the thoughts we entertain hold the pen. It isn't any
secret then, that our enemy would want to infiltrate our
thoughts in order to capture our imaginations. We must be
vigilant and discerning to see Satan for what he really is—
our enemy. His battleground is the mind.

[2] Matt. 6:25–34

"Imagination has the power to write
the scripts of our lives, and the thoughts we entertain hold the pen."

But Jesus comes that we might have life—and have it to the full.[3] We need to make sure he takes center stage. To do that, we need to not only recognize the enemy may be working behind the scenes, we need to be able to differentiate between his many voices.

Bill Johnson of Bethel church has often said, "Any area of my life for which I have no hope is under the influence of a lie."[4] The enemy speaks through many voices, and through them all, he inserts his lies. If we listen closely, we'll find his words devoid of hope. Here are just a few voices that can plant lies in our heads over time.

VOICES OF REGRET

I love Paul Manwaring's definition of regret:

"Regret is remembering your past without victories or value."[5]

---

[3] John 10:10
[4] Bill Johnson's Facebook page. Accessed December 27, 2011. www.facebook.com/BillJohnsonMinistries/posts/any-area-of-my-life-for-which-i-have-no-hope-is-under-the-influence-of-a-lie/10150449411323387/
[5] Manwaring, Paul. "Fully Present - Sunday PM." Bethel.TV, November 5, 2017. www.bethel.tv/watch/5029.

Regret has a way of keeping our minds in the past without any of the joys to cherish. Our past becomes a heavily weighted pile of "would haves" and "should haves" and nothing but bad decisions, indecisions, impulsive ideas, and defeats. Regret consistently directs our attention to the things that went wrong: You quit your piano lessons as a kid. You were too shy to try out for the basketball team. You never worked a decent job. In doing so, it blocks us from seeing the things that went right.

Regret tells your story in dark black marks, like a book written with a crude piece of charcoal that dirties your hands with each turn of the page. But if you dare look a bit harder at the memories of your past, you will discover victories, trophies, accomplishments, "firsts," and multiplied joys peppered throughout. Regret keeps us from noticing the good. It stunts our growth. We won't move on or excel if regret's voice leads the march through our imaginations.

THE VOICE OF SHAME

In her TED talk, Brené Brown discusses how guilt tells us we've done something bad, whereas shame tells us we are bad.[6] Shame accuses us of being irreparably flawed, broken, unlovely, and useless.

Shame's strategy is to keep our eyes cast down. It moves like a magnifying glass over our insecurities and relishes the ability to make us feel as small as possible. Narrating our pain and mistakes, shame says,

---

[6] Brené Brown, "Listening to Shame," filmed March 2012 in Long Beach, California, TED video, 20:38, https://youtu.be/psN1DORYYV0.

"None of this would have happened if you hadn't been you. You are the problem; your extinction is the solution."

Unlike regret, shame will find a way to make even our successes feel like burdens: You always get the attention; everyone must live in your shadow. Stop trying to be so big; you make others feel small.

Then it sets us up for rejection. It tells us that our successes or mistakes are the reasons we're despised or unloved—and we shouldn't expect any different. You see, it wants us to reject ourselves, to keep us from fully embracing the acceptance and grace of others.

When we give the voice of shame a foothold, it keeps us out of conversations, fellowship, friendship, and intimacy. It becomes the reason we struggle to make friendships, the reason we spend so much time alone. It becomes the reason we stop talking about our dreams and aspirations, the reason we stop trying to succeed, passing up opportunities to grow and be challenged.

Shame, like a gatekeeper, keeps many good things from flowing in and out of our lives. Famine is imminent when shame guards the gates.

THE VOICES OF COMPARISON, SELF-DOUBT, DISCOURAGEMENT, AND AN ORPHAN SPIRIT

If we venture to lift our heads after shame has said its piece, it won't take long for us to find other reasons to despair. To start, those of whom we're jealous will take center stage and the voice of comparison will have its say:

"You're not as smart as that one; you're not
as pretty as that one; and you're certainly
not as talented or competent as those."

Comparison uses a standard of measurement to which we
can never attain. As we struggle to reach each marker, the
benchmark moves further and further away. Before long,
we've adopted its voice and internally set unreasonable and
sometimes "not humanly possible" expectations for
ourselves.

Then self-doubt steps in, fueling our desire to give up
because we probably won't succeed anyway. Where
comparison shows us how far we must travel or change to
truly be someone, self-doubt deflates our tires before we
even begin trying.

And although we have family, friends, and meaningful
connections, the voice of the orphan spirit tells us we'll be
left all alone. Then it conjures up pictures of what that will
look like to be abandoned, at the mercy of evil, lack, and
injustice. With such thoughts, we can't help but panic.
Under the influence of this voice, we see resources as
scarce and help out of reach.

Then discouragement creates a chorus, calling to all the
disappointments of our life: poverty and struggles, neglect
and abuse, loss and betrayal, failure and defeat. He finds
the things that hurt the most, the things that marked our
lives in painful ways, and brings them to the forefront.

Like the taunting drums of an enemy army, these voices
join to threaten us and sing of our demise. Together, they
sing their songs in a concerto of dissonant chords with no
rests:

Comparison chants, "Don't even bother.
You cannot succeed!"

Shame intones, "There's nothing good in
you."

The orphan spirit plays the tune, "There is
never enough to go around."

And discouragement drones, "Your life is a
mockery, and it will never change."

Their verses contain the heroic deeds, possessions, and talents of those of whom you've felt bitter jealousy. They play the successes of others in fortissimo and leave your name out . . . always. Like the taunts of the army of Aram, the concert is intended for you, but every song leaves you lonely.

THE VOICE OF BLAME

Sometimes the siege isn't as much about pain as it is about how we view it. Specifically, what or whom do we view responsible for our trouble? When asked that question, the voice of blame likes to shift responsibility to something or someone other than ourselves.

"Sometimes the siege isn't as much about pain
as it is about how we view it."

When God came to Adam and Eve in the garden, after they had eaten from the tree of the knowledge of good and evil, he asked them what happened that caused them to hide. They each gave a different response: Adam blamed God for giving him the kind of woman (Eve) who would lead him into temptation, and Eve blamed the serpent for being cunning enough to fool her.

Notice Adam's phrasing of his answer:

> "The man said, 'The woman you put here with me—she gave me some fruit from the tree, and I ate it.'"[7]

His language puts distance between him and Eve by calling her "the woman;" and while he blames her, he ultimately blames God because he did, after all, "put her here."

Chances are good we've used (or seen someone use) a similar tactic: a child acts up, and rather than deal with the behavior, one parent says to the other, "Your son is behaving badly." Such language puts distance between the parent and child; it also distances one parent from the other.

And just like that, responsibility is shifted.

Ironically, because blame seeks to take the effects of our pain and create a metanarrative that shifts responsibility, it removes our authority for creating solutions or moving in the direction of hope and help. When we abdicate responsibility, we become disempowered. Blame says, "I am always the victim, therefore, my bad choices will always be someone else's fault."

[7] Gen. 3:12

Blame also binds us to a warped sense of justice. It wants a resolution that punishes others while giving us an excuse to be hurt, bitter, or tormented. Blame will not be satisfied even if true justice is served, because it causes us to believe our lives are already ruined, forever. It doesn't want us to venture into mercy or grace, because those two realities will render it powerless.

For the woman who gave up her child in 2 Kings, we can only imagine the voices that rang through her mind. Certainly, the echoes of the enemies that physically marched around the city, shouting threats, sparked her imagination. Watching neighbors and loved ones die of starvation surely suggested her son would share a similar fate, anyway. Watching her son suffer may have hinted that she'd be doing him a favor.

She was discouraged, orphaned, and hopeless. If only she knew her enemy was lying and that hope was within reach—she would not be known as the one who made a choice that destroyed a generation and forever scarred the conscience of two women and their king.

To break free from our own tragic tales, we need to find a way to question our thoughts before they become actions. We need to take our thoughts captive.

6

TAKING CAPTIVES

My mother used to quote Martin Luther, "You can't stop the birds from flying over your head, but you can keep them from building a nest in your hair." In other words, you can't stop all thoughts from coming into your mind, but you do have the authority to decide which ones get to stay. To do this, you need to take your thoughts captive and thoroughly examine them.

THE BROWN COW TECHNIQUE

A few years ago, a counselor friend of mine, Rick Bonnette, shared a story I will never forget:

> "Years ago, I had read a book about capturing the thoughts that run through our heads (2 Cor. 10:5). I struggled with this idea for a long time. It was an intimidating idea at first because of the flood of thoughts that occupied my own head. I felt as though it would be like trying to grab a speck of food out of a blender. My thoughts were random, lustful, angry, self-condemning, and fearful. I concluded, however, if the Lord tells us to do this, then it must be possible. As I prayed about this, the Lord gave me a picture.

In the vision there was a large pasture full of various cows grazing. There were brown ones, black ones, speckled ones, and red ones. There were hundreds of head of cattle as far as I could see. The Holy Spirit asked me, 'Rick, which cow is healthy?'

'I don't know, they are all out there wandering around,' I replied.
'What did you do back on the farm?' He inquired.
'Oh, well, we would round the cattle up into a holding pen,' I replied.

So, the next picture I saw in my mind was of the cattle holding pen.

'Which ones are healthy, and which are sick?' God asked.
'Now they are too closely packed, I can't really tell.' I said.
God persisted: 'What did you guys do after you rounded up the cattle into holding pens on the farm?'

'We would single out one cow and put them into a clamp to hold just one at a time and thoroughly examine it. Any sick ones would be directed to the barn for treatment and all the healthy ones we turned back out to the pasture where they could continue to eat and grow. The sick ones would be processed according to their needs.'

That's when the Holy Spirit began to tell Rick to pick out one cow and put it into the holding pen. Once that cow was in the pen, the Holy Spirit said to him, "Now thoroughly examine this one."

> "I began to just single out one thought at a time. I called it my "brown cow." As time went along, I began to get better at this.
>
> I quickly realized how weak and undisciplined my mind really had been. Before this lesson from the Lord, I would allow any thought to run through my head and I would accept it as true. This new practice began a new phase in my life. It wasn't long before I developed a system where I didn't just capture the fruit of my thoughts but could discern the actual origin of that thought/feeling.
>
> The Lord showed me that I will always grow negative fruit when there is a negative belief system about myself at the root. Colossians 3:9b says: 'Put away the old self [belief system] with its evil practices.'[1]

Rick then began to ask the Holy Spirit to show him throughout his day how many places that 'brown cow' lived; to his surprise, he discovered it in nearly every area of his life.

---

[1] Rick Bonnette, "Brown Cow. "Interview with Cate Morris, Email. June 13, 2018.

CAPTURING THOUGHTS

When I applied Rick's technique to my own life, I found my "brown cow" had worked its way into my life on many levels: "Your existence causes problems and pain for others." Through the voices of regret, shame, comparison, self-doubt, discouragement, and blame, I believed the real problem in life was *me.*

My mind ran through all the things I started and never finished. My enthusiasm to do new things or accomplish great things would always disappear when someone became jealous or pushed me away. Great things became things "I used to do." Good things were more tolerable. Doing nothing at all was easier still. I believed I created hardship for myself and everyone around me—as long as I was alive, I would create pain and shame for others as well as myself.

It wasn't true, of course. But up until the Holy Spirit pointed out this "brown cow," I believed it true. I assumed it was just my reality. My life decisions had all been affected by this way of thinking.

"Because God is fully committed to redeeming your life, he has already created solutions that provide hope and healing."

What about you? If you ask the Holy Spirit to help you identify the thoughts in your mind that did not originate with God, and find the task overwhelming, follow Rick's lead and asked God to point out the "brown" ones.

Because God is fully committed to redeeming your life, he has already created solutions that provide hope and healing. It's not up to you to heal; it's up to you to let God into your broken places so he can heal you.

THE VOWS WE MAKE AND CHOOSE TO BREAK

As we live and grow, we'll experience a multitude of joys, sorrows, disappointments, thrills, surprises, and adventures. With each experience, we decide whether to repeat it or make a change for the next go-round. These decisions become strategies and operating systems that govern our hearts and minds. Sometimes our responses are so strong they take the form of a vow.

Merriam-Webster defines a vow as: 1. v. To promise solemnly: swear; 2. To bind or consecrate by a vow.[2] When a thought begins with "I will never," it's likely you made a subconscious vow. Whether made as a child or as an adult, it's important to investigate; once you do, you'll likely expose more faulty thinking.

For me, as a teenager I decided I would never trust a man again. After watching the ups and downs and otherwise sabotaging behaviors of my father, after watching his inability to stick to his word to change, I decided all men must be the same and should not be trusted.

---

[2] Merriam-Webster.com Dictionary, s.v. "vow," accessed March 5, 2020, https://www.merriam-webster.com/dictionary/vow.

The problem with my self-preserving vow was that it wasn't based on complete information. My pain and struggle with *one* man caused me to picture that pain and struggle with *all* men. What made sense as a young adult clashed with the realities as an adult. I met several good men, great men, even—my husband being one.

The problem surfaced when I found myself in conflict with a man. It didn't even have to be a big issue, it just had to be uncomfortable. Once I felt the discomfort, fear crept in, and I was convinced I'd be made a victim or a fool. My adolescent vow was ready and in place to kick into gear, giving me cause to distrust, fear, and cut off relationships.

It was such a surprise to me when God began pinpointing my vows. These old operating systems had greatly bogged down my thinking and kept me from maturing in relationships where there was conflict. When my coping skills began flailing and faltering in relation to men, God began to ask,

"What are you believing right now?"

It didn't take long to pull up my beliefs, ideas, and thoughts on men. That file was so easily accessed in my mind, I identified those things right away.

"Men are untrustworthy, scary, and prone to hurt me," I replied.

"Is that true of all men, Cate?"

"It seems to be," I responded.

"What do you think of my evaluation of men? I called them 'good' you know."[3]

My response: I asked God to teach me how to see more than I'd been willing to see before. Because when God addresses our fear and pain, he also brings to light the habits and behavior we have developed to cope with that fear and pain.

One of the first unhealthy habits God pinpointed in me was sarcasm. For me, sarcasm made me a funny person (or so I thought); it also provided a sneaky way to cut someone before they could cut me. I was really good at it too.

Coinciding with my fear of men, sarcastic jokes about men rolled off my tongue with ease. I considered myself witty until God began to show me how I used sarcasm as a defense instead of communicating in vulnerability. If I feared I would not be heard or that my honesty would be trampled, I opted for sarcastic comments instead.

God asked if I would be willing to learn vulnerable communication instead of cutting people down with my words. I told him I would try. Sarcasm was so natural to me, I never considered it unhealthy until God put his finger on it. I needed God to point it out and draw my attention to it over the course of several months. He did.

Over the years I've become quicker at identifying my temptation to hurt others with words when I am afraid. Sometimes just biting my tongue and praying silently for God to help is my best course of action. Trusting God will help me even when I don't know how to help myself is one of the most beautiful lessons of faith I am learning.

[3] Gen. 1:31

This willingness to relinquish my ideas and vows in order to learn something more from the Lord becomes a surgery, much like a broken bone that has to be rebroken and set in order to heal properly. While scary, it ends up being such a blessing. Since the day God began dealing with this issue, I have been on a journey of replacing lies with truth, fear with trust, and intimidation with growing friendships.

Communicating truthfully is still scary at times. I still tremble when I know I need to speak up about my needs or the needs of others, but being a student to a more honest way of relating to others has reaped greater rewards. I no longer hurt others in order to self-preserve. I'm more approachable, trustworthy, and genuine. When I'm afraid in social situations, I ask the Holy Spirit to help me find my words, and he always does. I'll be a student of his ways for life.

The good news for me and for you is that God has made a way out of our futile thinking, and with his help we can operate from a different set of choices that originate in his heart. Hope, healing, redemption, and forgiveness all flow from him and are meant to reshape our lives by giving us all new options. We aren't at the mercy of our enemy as maybe we first believed.

7

THE GREAT ESCAPE

I n 2 Kings chapter 7, we're introduced to some new characters. Just outside the city of Samaria were four lepers. The Bible doesn't tell us the names of these men, but Jewish tradition suggests they were Gahazi[1] and his sons.

As was the law, they were not allowed to live within the city walls, since they had an infectious disease. There was famine inside the city, and famine outside the city, so the options for these men seemed to be death either way.

They were well aware of the fact they were unwanted and untouchable. Certainly, they heard words of rejection continually, and they lived the realities of it outside the city walls. They lived on borrowed time as it was, yet they did something surprising.

[1] Gahazi was a servant of the prophet Elisha. After Elisha cured Naaman of leprosy (2 Kings 5), Elisha refused payment. But Gehazi ran after Naaman and told him Elisha wanted a talent of silver. Naaman was so grateful for his healing, he gave Gehazi two talents. Because of his deceit, Elisha cursed Gehazi with the same disease from which Naaman had been healed.

They said to each other,

> *"Why stay here until we die? If we say,*
> *'We'll go into the city'—the famine is there,*
> *and we will die. And if we stay here, we will*
> *die. So, let's go over to the camp of the*
> *Arameans and surrender. If they spare us,*
> *we live; if they kill us, then we die."*
> *At dusk they got up and went to the camp of*
> *the Arameans. When they reached the edge*
> *of the camp, no one was there, for the Lord*
> *had caused the Arameans to hear the sound*
> *of chariots and horses and a great army, so*
> *that they said to one another, "Look, the*
> *king of Israel has hired the Hittite and*
> *Egyptian kings to attack us!" So, they got up*
> *and fled in the dusk and abandoned their*
> *tents and their horses and donkeys. They left*
> *the camp as it was and ran for their lives.*
> *The men who had leprosy reached the edge*
> *of the camp, entered one of the tents and ate*
> *and drank. Then they took silver, gold and*
> *clothes, and went off and hid them. They*
> *returned and entered another tent and took*
> *some things from it and hid them also. Then*
> *they said to each other, "What we're doing*
> *is not right. This is a day of good news and*
> *we are keeping it to ourselves. If we wait*
> *until daylight, punishment will overtake us.*
> *Let's go at once and report this to the royal*
> *palace." So, they went and called out to the*
> *city gatekeepers and told them,*

*"We went into the Aramean camp and no
one was there—not a sound of anyone—
only tethered horses and donkeys, and the
tents left just as they were." When King
Joram sent men to investigate the news that
the lepers brought back, he discovered the
truth of what was said, and that day the siege
of Samaria lifted.*[2]

Let that sink in for a minute . . .

Damned if they do, and damned if they don't, these men
decided that marching toward the enemy camp was just as
good of an idea as staying put outside the city walls. Death
would find them either way, but maybe this time they
would discover mercy, and they were willing to risk it all to
find out.

Despite the voices, rejections, and harsh realities in
which they found themselves, the lepers chose to look for
hope. They didn't deny their circumstances. They just
chose to change them.

The unwanted and unlovely, the rejected and repulsed
did something that no one else had tried. They allowed
hope to lead them into venture. They imagined a possibility
of grace and moved their lives in pursuit of it. And those
four lepers changed the course of history.

Scripture tells us with every step the lepers took, God
magnified and multiplied the sound, so their footfalls rang
out in a cacophony like an advancing army. Where four
lepers walked, their enemies heard chariots, horses, and
great armies. Their enemies fled in terror; and in their
haste, the army of Aram left the spoils of war behind where
it could be reclaimed by its rightful owners.

[2] 2 Kings 7:3–10

When the lepers arrived at the camp and realized the enemy was long gone, they knew they couldn't keep the news to themselves. There was a bounty in the camp for every survivor in Samaria. They quickly sent word back to their city that the siege was over, the enemy was gone, and there was food aplenty to eat.

CHOOSE HOPE

The lepers refused to let despair write their script. Their courage to dare resist the threats of the siege and move in hope for themselves became the catalyst of victory for an entire city.

When pain makes us feel as though we're in a lifeboat adrift at sea, by all means, we should pray for rescue; but we should also row for shore. We cannot make the mistake of throwing our oars overboard by shifting all responsibilities to someone else. There are things we can do right now.

Even if we're guilty of doing something that breaks God's heart, we can still move toward forgiveness, healing, wholeness, help, and freedom. Guilt is a signpost indicating a crossroads: today you choose.

And when we do move in the direction of hope and healing, the effects resonate beyond ourselves to our families, friends, neighbors, and even future generations. When we have been set free from the bondages of our enemy and we tell others about it, they can be free too.

But it is a choice.

Imagine if the two women from 2 Kings 5 chose hope as the lepers. Imagine if they had refused to give in to despair and decided to "go out to lunch." Imagine if they had put their babies on their hips and walked out of and away from the city.

You see, the hope the women in Samaria were so desperate for required leaving the siege to find. The same is true for you and me. Once we choose hope, we can't stay put; we must move toward that hope one step at a time. Let's get going!

8

HOPE THAT IS PRESENT

Here in Homer, Alaska, the economy is bolstered by tourism. Every week in the summer, cruise ships dock as motorhomes from around the world make their way to North America's most westerly highway point. For many tourists, visiting Alaska is on their "bucket list," and they're thrilled to be here.

To get the most of their Alaskan adventure, they'll often hire a guide service. Whether fishing, hiking, kayaking, hunting, or bear viewing, they want to experience the best Alaska has to offer.

A good guide knows the area: the weather, tides, layout of the land, animal habits, habitat, and history. A good guide always assesses the clients' abilities and prepares to make up for any lack; he carries the supplies or ensures they're prepared ahead of time to be in the right place at the right times. A good guide knows the best spots for the adventure being sought and where to get out of the weather if conditions turn sour.

Sometimes when we envision our lives (our futures, especially), our goal is just to somehow survive. We picture ourselves as if dropped off on a hostile island with just a guidebook full of parables and moral teachings we must interpret in order to live. When in truth, our lives are outfitted.

We've been dropped off on this planet with a guide— the Holy Spirit, who has so intertwined his life with ours, there is no way to be without him, unless we choose to disregard him. Through the Holy Spirit we have constant access to the resources and wisdom of God, but we must be willing to follow him and give his voice top priority.

It's imperative we walk daily with God, for he knows our future; he's scoped it out, laid supplies, cleared the path, and leads the way. Even if we don't know where we're going or what road will get us there, he does. He will see us through to our finish. Our successes will be the result of his abilities.

Because the Holy Spirit knows the end from the beginning, God can look at you and me and confidently say, "[I] who began a good work in you will be faithful to complete it until the day of my coming."[1] He has no doubts.

When we doubt, we need to refer to God's abilities— then commit ourselves "to him who is able to keep [us] from stumbling and to present [us] before his glorious presence without fault and with great joy."[2]

---

[1] Phil. 1:6
[2] Jude 1:24

FIX YOUR EYES

A few years ago, I had a dream. You know the kind of dream that makes you feel as though you learned something significant in your sleep? It was that kind of dream—a "God dream," I like to call it.

In the dream, I was traveling in an airplane with my children. At some point mid-flight, the captain's voice announced over the loudspeaker that the engines of the aircraft had failed and everyone on board needed to brace themselves for an emergency landing.

"our posture in pain or crisis determines
what we see"

As the flight attendants ordered us to put our heads between our knees, my children looked up at me in total fear. I looked at each of them in that moment and told them, "Jesus is on this airplane with us. Look for him." So, while the rest of the passengers had their heads down in the bracing position, my children and I were craning our necks looking around the cabin in search of Jesus.

Then I woke up.

That dream conveyed a valuable truth: our posture in pain or crisis determines what we see. If our eyes are on ourselves, or closed in fear, we'll miss the Prince of Peace—even though he's right beside us. The mere effort of looking for him in our pain or confusion activates our faith and moves us in the opposite direction of despair.

FOLLOW THE COMMANDER

One of my favorite excerpts from the book *The Shack* is a conversation Jesus has with the main character Mack. Jesus has some questions for Mack regarding whether people were designed to live in the past, the present, or the future. Mack answers:

> "I think the most obvious answer is that we were designed to live in the present. Is that wrong?"
>
> Jesus chuckled. "Relax, Mack; this is not a test, it's a conversation. You are exactly correct, by the way. But now tell me, where do you spend most of your time in your mind, in your imagination, in the present, in the past, or in the future?"
> Mack thought for a moment before answering. "I suppose I would have to say that I spend very little time in the present. For me, I spend a big piece in the past, but most of the rest of the time, I am trying to figure out the future . . ."

> ". . . Mack, do you realize that your
> imagination of the future, which is almost
> always dictated by fear of some kind, rarely
> if ever, pictures me there with you?"[3]

Too often the same could be said of us. Too often we let our imaginations have full reign and it depicts a tomorrow filled with hardship, struggle, pain, and fear . . . but no Jesus. The enemy excludes him on purpose—why? Because in Jesus "we have this hope as an anchor for the soul. Firm and secure. It enters the inner sanctuary behind the curtain . . ."[4]

The presence of God changes all our options. The help we didn't think available is within our reach: healing, forgiveness, supernatural strength, wisdom, and peace. He has promised he will never leave us or forsake us.[5] We can follow his lead because he is faithful.

God has always been in the stories. In our lives, in every season, in every siege, and in every victory he is ever-present. Our hope is not out of reach when we have the author of hope living within us.

God has said, "Never will I leave you; never will I forsake you."[6] We may not see him; we may have our head down, bracing for impact, but he's there. That's a promise. We will never be completely alone; it's impossible, because God is always there.

---

[3] William Young, The Shack (Newbury Park, CA: Windblown Media, 2007), 141–142.
[4] Heb. 6:19
[5] Deut. 31:6
[6] Heb. 13:5b

"When we let him turn on the lights in the dark room of our fears, all our negatives are exposed to his grace and hope."

With Jesus, tomorrow sure looks different. If we will keep our eyes on him, we'll see his power at work influencing life's outcomes, moving obstacles, and creating miracles. He is present in our fears and pain; he stays with us and clears a path. When we let him turn on the lights in the dark room of our fears, all our negatives are exposed to his grace and hope.

9

AMMUNITION

When it comes to fighting our enemy, we are not without ammunition. Jesus set the example for us by using the word of God as both a defensive and an offensive weapon against Satan. With it he corrected Satan's lies and rebuked Satan's threats. God's words in our mouth are powerful. We also have an arsenal of testimonies, proof of the goodness of God, that strengthens our faith. When we remember and declare what God has done, we celebrate the fact that he can and will do it again. God's victories for us and through us become banners that wave in the face of our adversary and infuse our hearts with hope.

> "When we remember and declare what God has done, we celebrate the fact that he can and will do it again."

The word of God is the most powerful weapon against our enemy. Speaking God's word is the most strategic weapon we can wield. It serves as a compass to help us find our direction when we are confused. It tells us the truth when we are being confronted with a lie, and it anchors us securely in the heart and character of God.

Jesus, when tempted by Satan in the wilderness to give up his destiny, refused to be manipulated and used the word of God as his defense:

> *Then Jesus was led by the Spirit into the wilderness to be tempted by the devil. After fasting forty days and forty nights, he was hungry. The tempter came to him and said, "If you are the Son of God, tell these stones to become bread. Jesus answered, "It is written: 'Man shall not live on bread alone, but on every word that comes from the mouth of God.'" Then the devil took him to the holy city and had him stand on the highest point of the temple. "If you are the Son of God," he said, "throw yourself down. For it is written, 'He will command his angels concerning you, and they will lift you up in their hands, so that you will not strike your foot against a stone.'" Jesus answered him, "It is also written: 'Do not put the Lord your God to the test.'" Again, the devil took him to a very high mountain and showed him all the kingdoms of the world and their splendor. "All this I will give you," he said, "if you will bow down and worship me." Jesus said to him, "Away from me, Satan! For it is written: 'Worship the Lord your God and serve him only.'" Then the devil left him, and angels came and attended him.*[1]

---

[1] Matt. 4:1-11

"It is written . . ." Each statement Jesus spoke began with the truth of the word of God, and that truth exposed the lies of the enemy. Notice, Jesus only had to speak one scripture to every lie the enemy threw his way. The truth of God stands alone; all other ideas are inferior to his word. Even Satan recognized this and was forced to back down.

"For the word of God is alive and active. Sharper than any double-edged sword, it penetrates even to dividing soul and spirit, joints and marrow; it judges the thoughts and attitudes of the heart. Nothing in all creation is hidden from God's sight. Everything is uncovered and laid bare before the eyes of him to whom we must give account."[2]

For every lie the enemy plants in our lives, we need a replacement truth. God's word is full of truth. That's why it's so important to delve into the treasure trove of Scripture and memorize passages that speak the truth. Here are a few examples . . .

When the enemy says, "You're all alone and you always will be," God's word says:

> *God is our refuge and strength,*
> *an ever-present help in trouble.*
> *Therefore, we will not fear, though the earth*
> *give way and the mountains fall into the*
> *heart of the sea, though its waters roar and*
> *foam and the mountains quake with their*
> *surging.*[3]

---

[2] Heb. 4:12
[3] Ps. 46:1–3

When the enemy says, "Your existence causes problems and pain for others," God's word says:

> *For you created my inmost being;*
> *you knit me together in my mother's womb.*
> *I praise you because I am fearfully and*
> *wonderfully made;*
> *your works are wonderful,*
> *I know that full well.*
> *My frame was not hidden from you*
> *when I was made in the secret place,*
> *when I was woven together in the depths of*
> *the earth. Your eyes saw my unformed*
> *body; all the days ordained for me were*
> *written in your book before one of them*
> *came to be.*
> *How precious to me are your thoughts, God!*
> *How vast is the sum of them!*
> *Were I to count them,*
> *they would outnumber the grains of sand—*
> *when I awake, I am still with you.*[4]

When the enemy says, "You've gone too far; there's no hope; God will never love you now," God's word says:

> *The Lord your God is with you,*
> *the Mighty Warrior who saves.*
> *He will take great delight in you;*
> *in his love he will no longer rebuke you,*
> *but will rejoice over you with singing.*[5]

---

[4] Ps. 139:13–18
[5] Zeph. 3:17

The word *rejoice* used here is a Hebrew word whose root means to exult and rejoice greatly, as one would celebrate at a wedding.[6] That's how God feels—in sheer delight he dances over us.

"learning to speak the truth out loud moves us from a passive acknowledgment of God's voice, to an active participant in his truth"

Of course, it's not enough to merely read these verses. After all, we are able to dismiss truth when feeling overpowered by a lie. But learning to speak the truth out loud moves us from a passive acknowledgment of God's voice, to an active participant in his truth. Speaking his words becomes a footstep out of our siege, and hope lights the way.

"Your word is a lamp for my feet, a light on my path."[7]

Say God's word out loud. Cause his words to speak louder than the voices taunting you, until they are quieted. Help is on the way.

[6] Blue Letter Bible, s.v. "Rejoice in Hebrew," accessed June 21, 2019, https://www.blueletterbible.org/lang/lexicon/lexicon.cfm?t=esv& strongs=h7797.

[7] Ps. 119:105

WAVE THE BANNERS OF VICTORIES PAST

Another powerful tool against the enemy is our testimony. The places where God has given us victory, insight, and wisdom are weapons in our hands against despair. When we begin to mine the rich treasure of our past for the things God has done, we'll find encouragement and strength to face the day. Mining my past, I find teachers, pastors, mentors, friends, and family members who encouraged me, prayed for me, wept with me, and believed in me. I recall their words, the times they invested in me, and the respite from pain they had been for me. I could see the goodness of God at work through the people in my life that he sent to love me through my pain.

I began to write down the testimonies of my life from the smallest of wins to the biggest victories. Praying, I asked the Holy Spirit to reveal to me memories long forgotten where he infused my life with hope and restoration, and I recorded each one on paper.

Once my list began filling up, I began reading them out loud. I read them to myself and then committed them to memory. I then began telling my stories to others. I made it a personal priority to recall the goodness of God and share it—certainly with my own family and children, but also with friends, neighbors, and even strangers. This was awkward at first because I was more used to talking about my problems than my victories; but the more I shared, the easier it became, and I found hope rising in me and hope rising in the hearts of those to whom I shared.

Like a banner waved in the face of our enemies, we need to choose to rehearse the good things God has done in our lives. When we feel a siege in full force, we need to declare God's goodness to our enemy and remind ourselves of what he has done. If God has done it before, he will do it again.

Our testimonies are powerful. Through remembrance, by declaring and celebrating, we keep God's goodness at the forefront of our thinking. This reorients our imaginations and keeps our hero, the Commander in Chief, at the helm of our battle.

Our enemy wants us to feel hopeless and trapped. He wants us to be suffering under the plagues of famine while he is feasting on the spoils of our inheritance. But he is a liar. We are not hopeless. We have hope, and we have weapons. Let's pick them up and reclaim what has been stolen. Read, memorize, and speak the word of God. Revisit, rehearse, and declare the goodness of God found in the testimonies of your life. Tell yourself, your children, your friends, your neighbors—and when in a siege, tell your enemy—what wonderful things the Lord has done.

10

VICTORY'S MARCH

It did not seem likely that four lepers from Samaria would share in a triumph for their entire city. Who would have thought it possible to leave the siege; who would have believed hope could be found outside the city walls? The very idea that their feet could sound like an army advancing against their enemy was not within the realm of human possibility—except God!

With God we have strength, courage, and triumph. And our triumph can become that of our neighbor if we will move from isolation to camaraderie. Combining our strengths and encouraging one another to keep going, we march together in the fight against our adversary. When we join our hearts and prayers, we share successes as well as struggles and our strength is multiplied.

Together, victory begins its triumphal march.

BUILD UP YOUR RESERVES

Another tactic of the enemy is to keep us so busy we have no time to spend in the presence of our Lord—because he knows the power it affords us.

Studying the Bible, memorizing Scripture, and seeking God's face when times are good helps build up our reserves for when times are bad.

A good way to get started is to find a local church that teaches the word of God and believes God is who he says he is according to Scripture. The local church is the extension of the body of Christ, and God equips them to serve and minister one to another. Just as our body needs many parts to function in health, God says the same thing about his body—the church. We are made up of many parts, and each part contributes to the health and encouragement of all.

While some may struggle to attend church because of the hypocrites who attend, I am so grateful! Even though my father was a broken man whose behavior worked to break his family, for whatever reason, he took us to church every week. We sat on the front row and participated in every church event.

Being a part of a local church introduced me to the presence of God. The liquid love and comfort of his Holy Spirit enveloped me at a very young age, and I knew I wanted to spend the rest of my life in his presence. It's what developed me into a worship leader, a revivalist, and a pursuer of the heart of God.

Of course, I have also come to realize the church can be as dysfunctional and unhealthy as the world. There are churches that preach the gospel as little more than a fairy tale, thus diminishing the power of God's word to the hearer; there are churches that use Scripture out of context, thus keeping its members captive under human power (cleverly disguised as God's direction); and there are churches that use "faith" as a badge of superiority, thus demeaning or otherwise attacking those who did not fit their preconceived mold.

Thankfully, we live in a technological world. Tools and resources—even live church services—are made available to us online.

And whether you are involved in a local church or plugged in virtually, make it a priority to spend time in God's presence every single day. Study your Bible, memorize Scripture (and seek to understand its context), and worship, with all your heart.

START MOVING

When we find ourselves in a siege, we need to listen to the Holy Spirit's prompting. Instead of accepting a fatalistic future, we need to put our "baby" on our hip and begin walking away from the thoughts of despair and hopelessness toward God's voice of mercy and hope.

Of course, I'm not talking a literal baby. "Put your baby on your hip" is a metaphor for realizing what is precious and worth fighting to preserve. That "baby" represents those things we're prone to throw away in great distress and prolonged duress. It could be a marriage, friendships, family, or even life itself. We need to take a good hard look at what we're tempted to give up on right now.

There are choices even amid hopelessness, so this moment is critical. Victory starts with a choice. Right now, there is hope and there is infinite help. Let us choose to grab everything we hold precious and get going.

Even as I write this book, the enemy's many voices threaten me. Self-doubt tells me I won't finish. Comparison tells me there are multitudes of books written on the subject I am writing and they are better. The orphan spirit tells me my story will change people's good opinions of me, and I will be abandoned. Shame tells me even if I succeed at finishing and publishing my book, it will make someone, somewhere, feel bad and they will let me know. But this is my story. With every word I type, I'm choosing to move in the direction of hope. Faith looks like movement.

It takes faith and courage to do the opposite of that which despair taunts us. We must believe God has another plan for us and that we can partner with him. We may not even be completely sold on the idea that God can help us. But when we move in his direction with our thoughts and actions, we discover his help and power along the way.

You may recall the man who brought his son to Jesus to be healed from convulsions, deafness, and dumbness. With faltering faith, the father asked Jesus if he could heal his son. Jesus responded by encouraging the man to believe in God's ability in all things. The man replied,

". . . I do believe; help me overcome my unbelief."[1]

His decision to go for help—even with weak faith—still produced a miracle. Jesus healed his son. Like the lepers whose weakness was met with God's strength, this man discovered what partnering with Jesus can do. I'm so glad Mark recorded the words of this man in his gospel. This story offers encouragement when we struggle to believe God wants to help.

[1] Mark 9:24

Once we're willing to take that first step toward hope, God infuses our steps with his supernatural power, making the enemy run in fear. Even if we feel our steps faltering or weakening, he joins them. With each step, he rewrites our story with his goodness and truth. We can say with confidence, "Surely goodness and mercy will follow me all the days of my life, and I will dwell in the house of the Lord forever."[2]

JOIN FORCES

Fred Rogers once said, "When I was a boy and I would see scary things in the news, my mother would say to me, 'Look for the helpers. You will always find people who are helping.'"

She was right. God may provide us a miracle that completely transforms our situations, but also, he'll send people to help, and their help becomes part of our miracle.

Just as our physical blood rushes to the location of our wounds in order to clean, fight for, and restore the broken part, God sends his people to be a part of our healing, rescue, and restoration. They are evidence of the mercy and love God extended to us. They may be professionals whom God has given wisdom; they may be people who have, at one time, stood where we're standing now. We need them to speak into our lives. They are the voice on the other side of a great bridge spanning the "unknown," coaxing us to the other side.

[2] Ps. 23:4

First, we need to open our eyes to the help being extended to us. We need to look for the resources God has placed in our lives—the counselors, pastors, doctors, and friends who have an interest in our healing.

Then we need to accept that help. When times get hard, it's all too easy to leave others outside our "walls," while we "eat our baby" in isolation. But it's vital that we keep in contact with those who are trying to help. We need to make those phone calls, keep those appointments, and follow up on those plans of rehabilitation.

The truth of the matter is, our enemy does not fly solo, and neither should we. We need our community of hope. Isolation can quickly become our enemy because it leaves us vulnerable.

The Bible says it this way:

> *Two are better than one,*
> *because they have a good return for their*
> *labor:*
> *If either of them falls down*
> *one can help the other up.*
> *But pity anyone who falls*
> *and has no one to help them up.*
> *Also, if two lie down together, they will*
> *keep warm.*
> *But how can one keep warm alone?*
> *Though one may be overpowered,*
> *two can defend themselves.*
> *A cord of three strands is not quickly*
> *broken.*[3]

---

[3] Eccles. 4:9–12

Of course, who we choose to partner with in our distress is critical (just look at the two drastically different outcomes from 2 Kings). We all have friends who are willing to tell us what we want to hear or give us quick solutions.

Destructive habits wait at the entrance of our hearts and minds and tempt us to try them. The temptation to go numb or to somehow avoid our crisis looks appealing, but the answer to walking out of our siege is going to take courage and require that we partner with wisdom.

CALL FOR BACKUP

Reaching out to others for prayer and help is one of the best things we can do when we choose to walk in victory. Because we can fall prey to the enemy's lies, it's important to create a "team" in every season of our lives.

Comprised of prayer warriors and people who walk in wisdom, your team should be chosen using the following criteria:

> 1. They must be trustworthy; you need to be able to be vulnerable and honest with them.
> 2. They must be willing to commit to pray for you and speak honestly to you.
> 3. You must commit to contact them when you are under siege.

My own team has been made up of pastors, other mothers, younger women who pray, counselors, and dear friends. Through the years, I've added to the team as others have moved on. This has been a life-saving commitment I have made to myself.

If I feel myself being pulled into a lie or struggling because I'm believing one, I call or text my team and ask them to pray for me. I don't have to give details, though I do when asked. They agree to pray for me the moment they receive my message, then we follow up with a phone call or meeting. My team does this for me, and I do this for them (and others). Having a team forces me to come out of hiding and gives me an action step.

Look around at the wise and prayerful people around you right now. Perhaps God will prompt them to be a part of your team for fighting against the lies of your enemy. If not, step out and begin asking.

Walking away from a siege is never easy. But our strength comes from the fact that we are constantly pursued by the goodness and mercy of God. We are not at the mercy of our enemy; for God says:

> *. . . do not fear, for I am with you; do not be dismayed, for I am your God. I will strengthen you and help you; I will uphold you with my righteous right hand. All who rage against you will surely be ashamed and disgraced; those who oppose you will be as nothing and perish. Though you search for your enemies, you will not find them. Those who wage war against you will be as nothing at all. For I am the Lord your God who takes hold of your right hand and says to you, do not fear; I will help you . . .* [4]

---

[4] Isa. 41:10–13

May this be true for you today. Right now, where you are, lift your head and expose your enemy. Put God's words in your mouth, put your baby on your hip, and start marching toward hope. Don't stop until your enemy is scattered and everything he has stolen is recovered. Do it for yourself. Do it for those you love. Do it for future generations.

Together, may our steps be the sound of a mighty army advancing against our enemy. May every siege be broken in the name of Jesus!

THE END

AFTERWORD

I've often wondered why this particular Bible story from 2 Kings became the story that arrested my attention. After all, I've never been tempted to eat my child, nor have I been starved to the point of insanity as people in this story had been. It was such a gross and obscure passage to me until that Sunday when God used it to question me.

My struggles have always been personal. As such, I believed no one else could be affected by them. I believed any harmful consequence of my decisions would only fall on me. This story showed me otherwise. This story taught me that no choices are made in a vacuum. No one suffers consequences alone.

By contrast, the story of the lepers depicts a better way. Together these stories of hopeless people showed me that the choices we make—whether good or bad—become the legacies of our lives.

It's been a long time since I found myself on the closet floor feeling overwhelmed and ready to give up. For that I am grateful. But it doesn't mean my enemy has removed his target from my head. He still sends his thoughts my way, but I recognize them now. My response time is much shorter than it used to be, and I have learned to turn my back on his "truths."

I don't speak his thoughts, and I quickly work to change the channel when my imagination begins playing his scripts.

My closet holds my shoes, my clothes, and my boxes of memoirs. When I need to put my baby on my hip and take a walk, I go to my closet to grab my shoes; I grab my phone and call or text my team and ask for prayer; then God and I go on a walk or a drive toward help and hope. I will continue in this new pattern for the rest of my life. I hope you will join me.

After all, fifty years from now, when future generations ask whether God is real, it will be your story and mine they reflect on to make their decisions. Let us be determined to leave a treasure trove of his goodness as our legacy.

NOTES

Opening

Merriam-Webster.com Dictionary, s.v. "siege," accessed March 9, 2020, https://www.merriam-webster.com/dictionary/siege.

Chapter 1: The Siege Begins

1. Morris, Cate. "Pass It On." *The Musings of Cate Morris*, 14 Mar. 2016. https://catemorris.com/2016/03/04/pass-it-on.

Chapter 2: Famine in the Land

2. 2 Kings 6:24 (NIV)
3. Shekel. Conversion Chart / Historical Weights Units Converter, Biblical. Accessed March 9, 2020, https://www.convert-me.com/en/convert/history_weight/bibshekel.html?u=bibshekel&v=80.
4. "What Are the Biblical Weights and Measures in Modern Terms?" CompellingTruth.org. Accessed March 9, 2020. https://www.compellingtruth.org/biblical-weights-and-measures.html.

5. "Seed pods," also "dove dung," depending on the Bible translation.
6. 2 Kings 6:25
7. Deuteronomy 28:49–57
8. 2 Kings 6:26–30
9. *Merriam-Webster.com Dictionary*, s.v. "despair," accessed March 9, 2020, https://www.merriam-webster.com/dictionary/despair.

Chapter 3: AWOL

10. Genesis 1:27; Genesis 2:7
11. Genesis 1:28
12. It's generally believed that one third of heaven's angels fell, based on Revelation 12:4: "And his tail swept away a third of the stars of heaven, and threw them to the earth. And the dragon stood before the woman who was about to give birth, so that when she gave birth, he might devour her child."
13. Hitchcock, Roswell D. *An Interpreting Dictionary of Scripture Proper Names.* New York, N.Y., 1869.
14. Elwell, Walter A. *Evangelical Dictionary of Theology.* Ada, Michigan: Baker Academic, 1997.
15. John 8:44b
16. Rhodes, Ron. "How Did Lucifer Fall and Become Satan?" Christianity.com. Salem Web Network, October 22, 2007. https://www.christianity.com/theology/theological-faq/how-did-lucifer-fall-and-become-satan-11557519.html.

17. Stafford, Wess, and Dean Merrill. *Too Small to Ignore: Why Children Are the Next Big Thing.* Colorado Springs, CO: Waterbrook Press, 2005.
18. Zacharias, Ravi. Twitter post. June 22, 2014, 8:18 a.m. https://twitter.com/ravizacharias/status/480731662834475008?lang=en.
19. Ephesians 2:10
20. Romans 3:23 KJV
21. Genesis 3
22. Romans 6:23 KJV
23. Genesis 25:29–34
24. 2 Corinthians 10:5

Chapter 4: Recognizing Our Enemy

25. Ephesians 6:12
26. Genesis 3
27. Kolenda, Daniel. "Be Saved from this Perverse Generation, Azusa Now Livestream- Last 4 Hours English." *YouTube video*, 2:48, posted by Content Global, May 24, 2016, www.youtube.com/watch?v=5L7q8fYuQao.

Chapter 5: Deciphering the Truth

28. *Merriam-Webster.com Dictionary*, s.v. "imagination," accessed March 9, 2020, https://www.merriam-webster.com/dictionary/imagination. www.merriam-webster.com/dictionary/imagination?src=search-dict-box.
29. Matthew 6:25–34

30. John 10:10
31. Johnson, Bill. 2011. Facebook, December 27, 2011.
    www.facebook.com/BillJohnsonMinistries/posts/any-area-
    of-my-life-for-which-i-have-no-hope-is-under-the-
    influence-of-a-lie/10150449411323387.
32. Manwaring, Paul. "Fully Present - Sunday PM."
    Bethel.TV, November 5, 2017. www.bethel.tv/watch/5029.
33. Brown, Brené. "Listening to Shame," filmed March 2012
    in Long Beach, California, TED video, 20:38,
    https://youtu.be/psN1DORYYV0.
34. Genesis 3:12

Chapter 6: Taking Captives

35. Bonnette, Rick. "Brown Cow." Interview with Cate Morris.
    Email. June 13, 2018.
36. 2 Corinthians 10:5
37. Colossians 3:9b paraphrased by Rick
38. *Merriam-Webster.com Dictionary*, s.v. "vow," accessed
    March 5, 2020, https://www.merriam-
    webster.com/dictionary/vow.
39. Genesis 1:31

Chapter 7: The Great Escape

40. Hitchcock, Roswell D. *An Interpreting Dictionary of
    Scripture Proper Names*. New York, N.Y., 1869.
41. Isaacs, Jacob. "Samaria Under Siege," *Kehot Publication
    Society* (January 24, 2007),
    https://www.chabad.org/library/article_cdo/aid/464002/jew
    ish/Samaria-under-Siege.htm.
42. 2 Kings 7:3–10

Chapter 8: Hope That is Present

43. Philippians 1:6
44. Jude 1:24
45. Young, William P. *The Shack*. Newbury Park, CA: Windblown Media, 2007.
46. Hebrews 6:19
47. Deuteronomy 31:6
48. Hebrews 13:5b

Chapter 9: Ammunition

49. Matthew 4:1–11
50. Hebrews 4:12
51. Psalm 46:1–3
52. Psalm 139:13–18
53. Zephaniah 3:17
54. Blue Letter Bible, s.v. "Rejoice in Hebrew," accessed June 21, 2019, https://www.blueletterbible.org/lang/lexicon/lexicon.cfm?t=esv&strongs=h7797.
55. Psalm 119:105

Chapter 10: Victory's March

56. Quote by Fred Rogers. Goodreads. Accessed March 9, 2020, https://www.goodreads.com/quotes/198594-when-i-was-a-boy-and-i-would-see-scary.
57. Mark 9:24
58. Psalm 23
59. Isaiah 41:10–13

RESOURCES

Cate's blog site is www.catemorris.com, and her ministry site is www.runtomercy.com.

Cate Morris's music can be downloaded from Amazon.com and iTunes and is available for sale through www.cdbaby.com.

ABOUT THE AUTHOR

Meet Cate...

Worship leader, singer, songwriter, preacher, and teacher, Cate Morris grew up in Boise, Idaho. After graduating from Christ for the Nations Institute in Dallas, Texas, in 1995 after graduating, she began ministering in her hometown and in various mission fields around the world through preaching and music ministry. After marrying her husband, Jamin, Cate moved to Alaska, where she based her ministry.

Today, Cate teaches Apologetics and Worship at the Alaska Bible Institute in Homer, Alaska; she also teaches and leads worship for churches and conferences nationally and internationally. Her ministry to women, youth, and worship leaders bridges denominations as she encourages through song, testimony, preaching, teaching, and heartfelt worship.

Cate currently resides in Homer, Alaska, with her husband, Jamin, and their four children—Bethany, Jaron, Chad, and Melanie. She has released two albums: *From Here* and *Red Sky*.

www.ingramcontent.com/pod-product-compliance
Lightning Source LLC
LaVergne TN
LVHW041233080426
835508LV00011B/1187